Insights

CONSUMER BEHAVIOUR, MARKETING & MORE

NIMISH RUSTAGI, Ph.D.

This book is dedicated to my mother Dr Urmila Rustagi who keeps blessing me from the heavens, my father T R Rustagi,
my wife Anubhuti – my pillar of strength,
my kids Neer & Saavi –for keeping me grounded, literally.
Thanks for your unwavering support, love and understanding.

CONTENTS

Prologue

Consumer behaviour is a fascinating subject that has captured the attention of marketers, advertisers, and business owners for decades. However, despite its importance, there is still a lot that is not commonly known about this complex and multi-faceted field.

This book aims to shed light on some of the lesser-known insights on consumer behaviour and marketing that can help not just marketing managers to better understand their customers, but also help an everyday consumer understand some simple ways to become a happier consumer.

Through 12 independent and standalone chapters that are backed by solid research, the book delves into different areas of consumer behaviour, marketing and more.

The issues taken up for discussion include –retail therapy and whether it can help to restore a consumers' low sense self-worth, how can consumers plan their money spend to get more happiness from consumption, how choice impacts well-being of consumers, how a consumer's expertise in a product could become a bane.

There are other chapters focusing on the impact of the pandemic on consumer behaviour and marketing. Here, the discussion centres on issues of branding, consumption trends, psychology of consumers, and converging retail models in the face of unprecedented crisis.

The book also delves into contemporary issues and trends such as, the spread of the selfie culture, blockchain technology and its use for education, green businesses and imperatives for achieving sustainable development.

1. Retail therapy, does it repair a consumer's self-worth?

As shopping trends peak over festive seasons, Christmas, Diwali, Eid, they are also timely moments to gauge the effects of a kind of retail therapy that researchers call compensatory consumption – but one that has a non-conscious process behind it.

Indeed, why precisely do consumers buy products that they don't really need? And if shopping is supposed to be therapeutic, to what degree is such consumption helping them to deal with their insecurities?

Most importantly, once they buy the product, does that purchase actually make them feel better?

These are the questions which drove the research we conducted from 2015 to 2018, absorbed as we were by the hidden impulses driving people's consumption choices.

What we discovered is that certain marketing tactics, associated with forms of consumption, including the ones we see around festival times, might adversely impact consumer well-being. By bringing these findings to the fore we hope they can help consumers understand and rein in emotional impulses that drive their shopping.

The Festive Shopping Drive

Surveys reveal that the festivals and end-of-year holidays encourage a degree of collective over-consumption and binge shopping rarely seen at any other times of the year.

Despite the moderating effects of COVID-19 pandemic, data from the The National Retail Federation reveals that during 2022 more than 196 million consumers in the United States shopped in-store and online between Thanksgiving and Cyber Monday. According to some estimates, shoppers in the United States, spent an average of US$870 on their Christmas gifts in 2022. For American retailers, meanwhile, Christmas represents the year's largest economic stimulus.

Similar trends are discernible in India during the Diwali festival season. During 2022 for instance, it is estimated that Indians shopped for over US$ 27 billion during the few weeks from September to November, with the volumes split between offline and online consumption. Such trends are reflected elsewhere across the world as people spend excessively not just at Christmas or Diwali but pretty much on every occasion that motivates consumption.

These shopping sprees take in the November 11 Singles' Day and Lunar New Year in China; the end-of-year holidays travels in the region; and the year-end bonuses in Japan, South Korea, Taiwan

Non-Conscious Drive To Consume

Among these consumers are people unconsciously seeking to boost a damaged self-worth (their power, intelligence, or even sociability). This compensatory consumption is a well-documented impulse, an action arguably becoming more widespread as consumption becomes available 24/7, thanks to the services on Internet.

So, when Sophie (not her real name), discovers her project's funding had been slashed by her boss, she suddenly becomes enamoured by the Bottega Veneta leather bag advertisement in her favourite fashion magazine. Meanwhile, after failing his engineering course, Phillip's first instinct is to buy a marble chess set he never previously dreamt of splurging on.

Both have been drawn into compensatory consumption, which aims to fix damaged aspects of self-identity.

Sophie seeks a product symbolic of status and power, to regain her sense of power. Meanwhile, Phillip's interest in a chess set that is symbolic of intelligence is driven by his need to affirm his intellectual capacity.

Crucially, both are unlikely to be aware of the drivers behind their interest in these products.

(Photo: Unsplash/Heidi Fin)

Explicit Versus Implicit Marketing

But does consumption really manage to repair their self-worth? We explored the effects of compensatory consumption on self-worth in the US, France and India.

Concomitantly, we analysed what effect marketing tactics have on this retail therapy. Across seven experiments involving over a thousand volunteers, our research reveals that whether compensatory consumption works to fix people's damaged sense of self-worth depends on the extent to which the connection between the products and aspects of the threatened self-identity is made explicit.

Our conclusions, recently published in Journal of Consumer Research, give us pause for thought.

Yes, consumers compensate for their "self-deficit" by purchasing goods they may not consciously need. However, if brands incite connections to their "self-deficit" in an explicit manner, through their products' names or marketing slogans, this "compensatory" effect is impeded, even at a subconscious level.

When Sophie is tempted by the Bottega Veneta leather bag, its tagline, "When your own initials are enough", spells out the product's connection with power, which is the damaged aspect of her self-identity but might undermine her process of self-repair.

Phillip's unconscious desire to repair his insecurities about his intelligence through purchasing the chess set could be undermined if the makers use and remind him of slogans like that coined by the 17th century French philosopher Blaise Pascal: "Chess is the gymnasium of the mind".

In both cases, these explicit messages will remind Sophie and Phillip about their respective failures of power and intelligence, and rumination will impede repair of self-worth.

However, our research also reveals that when connections between the product and "self-deficit" are not explicit, it increases the chances for self-repair. Sophie might well restore her self-worth, for example, by splurging on the Bottega Veneta leather bag if there are no taglines explicitly associating it to aspects of power, as luxury products inherently and implicitly symbolise and boost feelings of power and status.

(Photo: Unsplash/freestocks)

Shopping With A Sting

This outcome is not limited to luxury goods alone; it can apply to any goods that symbolise an aspect that a shopper feels strongly about. So, a mere subscription to an intellectual magazine with an explicit tagline could also re-activate negative feelings about one's own intelligence.

Our research outlines the conditions in which this form of consumption can restore the damaged self. It also questions the marketer's belief that taglines about the attributes of a brand or product is beneficial for consumers seeking to associate themselves with those attributes.

In conclusion, compensating through consumption of products with explicit marketing could have the insidious effect of actually prolonging rather than repairing the damaged self-concept.

So, in this high-octane festive period, should you feel, like Sophie and Phillip, an unexplainable urge to buy a fancy leather bag, high-brow chess set, Rolex watch, upmarket pen, speedy car, or any other symbol of self-worth, you should pause and think again.

Just what is driving this impulse? Should the desire be linked to a life experience that has shaken your confidence, perhaps your purchase will not repair the damage you are trying to overcome – quite the opposite.

(This is an updated and revised version of an article first published on ChannelNewsAsia.Com in December 2018 and is based on the research work of Nimish Rustagi and L. J. Shrum that was originally published in the Journal of Consumer Research in 2018)

2. Why you should spend your money on experiences, not things

The ad breaks grab my thirteen-year-old son's attention much more than the cartoon series he watches on TV. He wants to have every product that engages him through compelling marketing pitches dominating his chosen media. In one way or another, the same story holds true for so many of us inhabiting the marketing world; rightly or wrongly, we all would love to have it all.

But alas! Unless you are the famous founder of a big tech firm from Silicon Valley or someone who owns a multi-story house piercing through the Mumbai skyline, you would probably have limits to your budgets and thus forced to prioritise your consumption. Given the limits to the kitty at your disposal, your strategic goal should be to spend your pennies to maximise your well-being or happiness.

Given that you always have multiple needs, how should you prioritise your spending in order to maximise your consumption-derived well-being? Should you buy that luxury dress you have been eyeing for sometime? Or, should you finally take that Himalayan trek that you have been planning? Or, should you pick up that electric guitar to practise your favourite tunes?

Consumer psychologists throw some light on the types of consumption and the extent of well-being that may accrue to the consumers. In general, consumers are better off investing in life experiences rather than material possessions as positive life experiences tend to provide greater well-being.

If you spend your precious pennies on taking that Himalayan trek, it is likely to bring you rich well-being dividends. Compared to material possessions, investing in life experiences result in greater well-being. Experiences lend themselves better to subjective interpretations that become increasingly positive over time – as time passes, we sub-consciously de-emphasise the negative elements of our experiences thereby focusing only on the positive ones, and such life experiences are also inherently social; they are often lived, shared or recalled in the company of others. Surely you would love to tell your friends and colleagues tales from your Himalayan trek as well as fondly remember the moments you shared with others during the trek. To summarise, our life experiences better satisfy our psychological needs of self-expression and our fundamental need to connect with other human beings. Therefore, do invest in gaining life experiences such as eating out with your loved ones, going for a concert and travelling -- they are a key to your happiness and well-being, and that too, over extended periods of time.

Hey, but would you be worse-off if you were to buy that electronic guitar rather than opting for the trek? Let us de-construct the guitar. Though it is a material product, it also has an intangible element to it – that of being an enabler of an experience of learning and playing music. Same would perhaps be true of other experience enabling products such as videogames, a 3D television, sporting goods and so on. All such products help create and enable distinct life experiences. Research by Darwin A. Guevarra from University of Michigan and Ryan T. Howell from San Francisco State University found that such 'experience products' may also generate as much consumer well-being as intangible life experiences. Much like non-material life experiences, such experience products also lend themselves to positive recollections and enriching social engagements borne out of the experiences enabled by them. You are quite likely to cherish playing your favourite tunes, and recollect those musical evenings and social engagements made possible by the guitar.

That leaves us with examining the possibility of you purchasing that much-longed-for luxury dress. Oh God, you really want to have it. Most often material products, such as clothing, jewellery and accessories are purchased with the intention 'to have' as opposed 'to do'. Purchases rooted in such intentions tend to emerge from and result in social comparisons or comparison with other products, and such extrinsic concerns can undermine a consumer's well-being. Further, consuming such products may not result in social benefits such as those provided by life experiences (e.g., Himalayan trek) and experience products (e.g., electric guitar). It is not that material consumption cannot make us happy -- it may, but investing in life experiences or experience products is likely to bring us superior well-being returns.

Where does this leave you and me? A better understanding about the value of experiences embedded in consumption might help some of you to better draw or revise your spending list. As for me, the next time my son demands a new pair of jeans, a tennis racket and a visit to the zoo, I know as to which of his demands I shall give in at first.

(This is an updated and revised version of an article first published on cnbctv18.com in July 2019)

3. Spoilt for choice: Why more is not always better for consumers

Having a coffee was never such a complex exercise in decision-making. The other day, the barista at the upscale coffee bar stumped me with a list of exotic cappuccinos, when all that I wanted was simply a cup of nice hot cappuccino. Truly, we live in an era of choices.

(Photo: Unsplash/Franki Chamaki)

The supermarket aisles are full of a whole range of chocolates, breads, chips and cereals. Universities and colleges offer prospective students a wide range of courses to choose from. Insurance sellers, matrimony portals, car dealers and banks provide us choices like never before. It seems as if, the law of the land is to offer as many options as possible to consumers who value having maximum choice. Having a choice is consistent with the much-cherished values of freedom, democracy, self-expression and autonomy.

Few would contest that having more choice is better than having less of it. This widespread belief is also supported by the Rational Choice Theory in economics. A rational consumer wants to maximise his or her utility from making a choice and a wider set of options provides a better opportunity to do just that. And indeed, well-educated consumers and the super-smart millennials are rational. They want the best and so they explore as many options as possible. Psychologists too contend that exercising choice enhances an individual's sense of personal control and feelings of autonomy. No wonder '*Yeh Dil Maange More Choice*'. An increasing number of consumers are becoming what Barry Schwartz terms as 'maximisers'. Nothing but the best works for them and thus they choose only after examining maximum possible options. Moreover, the diffusion of e-commerce, online sellers and internet-enabled tools has made product comparison much easier, further fueling the maximiser mindset.

Stiff Competition

This trend has been captured as well as strengthened by product manufacturers and sellers. Manufacturers, retailers and supermarkets are locked in a stiff competition to provide more choices to the consumer. Mega shopping malls as well as online sellers wish to stand out from the crowd based on the variety, options and choice they offer. As consumers, it is common for us to prefer a shopping mall that offers greater choice, whether the product we seek be home furnishings, electronics, apparel or groceries. Offering widest possible choice assures the store managers of a higher footfall, which they believe translates into higher sales and profitability.

However, the story of choice is perhaps a more nuanced one. Having and exercising choice is indeed great. But how much of choice is good, is the question. When consumers choose amongst a manageable number of options, it is likely to bring positive rewards in terms of the satisfaction that the exercise of rational choice brings. Making a selection from a manageable set of alternatives also enables consumers to experience feelings of autonomy and freedom. However, when the options to consider are too many, making a choice can have a negative effect on consumers' well-being.

Research shows that choosing from a very wide set of options drains the consumer psychologically. Choice overload can produce decision-making paralysis, depression and low-satisfaction with the choice finally made. Such consumers are likely to choose a product without an exhaustive scanning of all available options. This can make them less confident and sure about their own choices. Consequently, they are more likely to experience post-choice regret. They are likely to question their own choices (say, a designer bag) and indulge in comparison with choices made by others (say, a different designer bag bought by a friend) or with options that they did not choose (other designer bags that were available). Clearly, too much choice can dampen consumer well-being.

In contrast, when consumers choose a product from a smaller and manageable number of options, they process information about each available option more actively and then make their choice. Such consumers have greater confidence in their choices and tend to be more satisfied with their selection. Studies by psychology professors Sheena S. Iyengar and Mark R. Lepper, from Columbia and Stanford University respectively attest to this understanding. They also show that consumers are unaware of the linkages between the number of options they consider and its psychological impact on them. Instead, consumers report greater enjoyment with the decision-making process when they are provided more options to choose from; even though they find choosing among too many options both difficult and frustrating.

A Manageable Number of Options

It seems a consumer is better-off choosing from a smaller and manageable number of options. But what is this optimal and manageable number? This number will depend on the type of product, its price and its importance to the consumer. For instance, the number of homes one may consider before buying one is likely to be different than the number of options one considers while picking a standard grocery item. As a general rule though, a consumer is better-off choosing from a set of options that is manageable in size rather than one which offers excessive options. However, consumers are not always aware of the curse of excessive choice. Only a few learn to happily choose a 'good enough' rather than 'the best' option from a manageable number of relatively fewer alternatives while paying little attention to what others around may be doing. No wonder, most consumers still prefer stores and shopping malls that offer them far more than the manageable number of options to choose from.

What about sellers and stores? Should they continue to offer consumers the maximum possible options to choose from? The studies above also suggested that consumers who consider products from a smaller and manageable choice set are more likely to eventually buy the product compared to those considering from an extensive choice set. Thus, sellers and stores would be better off optimising the number of options they offer in each product category. Blindly offering the most extensive choice-set in each product category may result in higher inventory costs and lower sales and that too alongside a psychologically drained and dissatisfied consumer. Stores and sellers should rely on credible research to work out the optimal range of products to keep. While the footfall in a shopping mall may still depend on the extensiveness of the choices it offers, it may not achieve the most optimal 'sales to footfall' ratio or the best possible profitability.

Well, I could finally get my cappuccino. Perhaps, the customers and sellers too could indulge in their cappuccinos to reflect upon the choices they have.

(This is an updated and revised version of an article first published on cnbctv18.com in November 2019)

4. The truth about shopping --twist in the tale

If a slogan could find appeal around the world it would perhaps be 'Hail Shopping'. We live in a world dotted with mega malls and 24x7 online stores, countless once-in-a-lifetime special offers and ever-persuasive advertising.

It seems that no longer one needs a good reason to grab those ever-enticing products, as the love of shopping in itself is a reason enough to splurge. Erma Bombeck once said that the odds of going to the store for a loaf of bread and coming out with only a loaf of bread are three billion to one. Her words sum up the power of materialistic world – seems we just can't resist it nor can we have enough of it.

During the 2022 Diwali season, we Indians spent an estimated Rs 1.75 lakh crore (US $ 20 billion) on just the offline shopping.

Among the top buying categories were smart phones, large appliances, furnishing fabrics and fashion products. And yes, these are the estimated figures from just the offline shopping.

Increased consumer spending is hailed as good news for the economy as it fuels business activity, job and wealth creation. Yet, we all know of elders and wise ones in our families warning us not to pamper or spoil the kids by fulfilling all their worldly wishes. After all, they need to realise the value of hard-earned money and also learn to conserve and value what they already possess.

Psychologists too are wary of increasing materialism, defined by Marsha Richins, Professor at University of Missouri, as a personal value that reflects the importance consumer places on the acquisition and possession of material objects. A materialistic person believes that having products brings happiness and is a marker of success. Further, materialism defined as such has been widely measured with a psychometric scale developed by Marsha Richins and Scott Dawson. Research across cultures suggests that highly materialistic people tend to have lower self-esteem, life satisfaction and well-being, stronger feelings of loneliness, positive attitudes towards borrowing and a greater probability for indebtedness. A vast amount of research suggests that as human-beings seek to make more and more money, want to buy more, acquire more and possess more, they are perhaps treading a tunnel of doom with no light at the end.

But hey, let us pause and reflect. There must be something good for us in our quest for financial success and in all that shopping we do with that money. After all, we do experience joy and happiness when we possess that new house and when we get together for that family dinner at the newly opened eatery. So here is the twist in the tale. We must assess our consumption along with the motivation behind it. It is the motives behind our apparently materialistic pursuits that determine whether they result in doom or boon. Research shows that when our motives for a particular purchase or possession are extrinsic in nature, such as to gain social approval from others, such consumption may not enhance our psychological well-being. However, when the primary motives behind our consumption are intrinsic, such as, to ensure safety and security of ourselves or our loved ones, to support our family, to self-express or to reflect our core values, such consumption enhances our overall well-being. Thus, buying an expensive new house in a prime city locality or spending a fortune on a family dinner at the top-rated restaurant may enhance our well-being when the primary motivation behind these actions is an intrinsic one, for instance to ensure a more secure or peaceful neighbourhood to live in or to derive joy from spending quality time with our dear ones.

Be rest assured that all that shopping on Diwali eve was not all in vain; perhaps much of it was to express our love, gratitude and appreciation for those others in our lives or reflect our own core values such as our creative or geeky streak. It is not that our marketers do not know these fundamentals of consumer well-being. Why else do you think the greatest brands of our times are built around aspects that are fundamentally intrinsic to us, and thereby instigating us to Think Different or to Just Do It!

(This is an updated and revised version of an article first published on cnbctv18.com in June 2019)

5. Are you a wine sommelier? A consumer with deep knowledge? Be wary of the emotional costs of expertise!

All of us crave to consume things and live the experiences that make us feel good. These are things and experiences, an indulgence with whom, promises to bring us emotional joys and positive feelings. Savouring a glass of wine, listening to music, watching films, clicking the camera to capture that perfect moment, blissfully devouring an ice-cream or buying that latest fashion jewellery – all these and many more behaviours elicit our positive emotions and thereby make us feel good.

Given such consumption's positive trade-offs, it is natural that many consumers are motivated to take their consumption experience to the next level. These consumers want to learn more about the subtleties and nuances of the products that fill them with positive emotions. For instance, a movie buff wishing to become a more discriminating cinephile, may enrol in a course to acquire expert knowledge on different aspects of film making. For such aspirational expert-film-consumers, short courses are offered – now purely online ones too - by film institutes, such as Film and Television Institute of India (FTII). Similarly, those who enjoy music, photography or wine, often aspire to develop certain level of expertise in their much-loved product, skill or hobby.

It is not unusual nor uncommon to find consumers pursuing knowledge and expertise on things that bring them an emotional high or joy. Indeed, they do so in the firm belief that greater expertise would result in further enriching their consumption-derived positive feelings and experiences.

Acquiring expertise is a rewarding endeavour. With expertise come benefits such as more efficient information processing, better memory of relevant information and even better decision making.

(Photo: Unsplash/Austin Distel)

Acquisition of extensive knowledge within a product domain or a field (e.g., wine, coffee, music, photography) enables consumers to apply an analytical approach to understand product domains and fields and make more rational evaluations. For instance, an expert in photography shall assess a set of photographs based on elements such as composition, light and angles. Much the same way, a whiskey sommelier, would discriminate between whiskies by dissecting them on aspects of complexity, balance, smoothness, finish and so on. There are other candies too for being an expert. One may feel proud of one's expertise – such as the film buff with a well-earned FTII certificate. Mastery in a product domain may also render an enhanced social prestige – remember how we are in awe of people amidst us who seem to know all about music. Moreover, experts such as gourmet reviewers on the Instagrams and Pinterests of the world, get a chance to cherish their popularity as well as the free food tasting invites, they receive from exciting food joints and bistros.

We may wonder whether there is more to the glorious and grand story of being an expert-consumer. Specifically, is there a possible twist in this tale? It seems, there is.

The above question was studied by consumer researchers Matthew D. Rocklage, Derek D. Rucker and Loran F. Nordgren from University of Massachusetts, Boston and Northwestern University. Their research, published recently in the Journal of Consumer Research, shows that having expertise in certain product domains and fields can make such expert-consumers emotionally numb.

That is, such expert-consumers display and experience less intense emotions when they consume certain products which are consumed primarily to provide hedonic thrills based in positive feelings and emotions. The products such as wine, fine gourmet, movies, photography, beer and music fall in this category.

When experts engage with a product or consume it, they tend to evaluate and assess the product and their consumption experience by employing their expert knowledge on the product. Using an analytical approach, they dissect the product into its constituent parts to make conclusions about the product.

However, when this default analytical approach is adopted for hedonic products and fields, of the kind mentioned above, it leads the expert-consumers away from experiencing the spontaneous feelings and pure emotions, that say a non-expert consumer or a novice would derive from consuming such products. Let us try to visualise these findings.

Imagine, you drop into a winery to enjoy a Chardonnay. Remember, your goal is to enjoy a glass of Chardonnay, perhaps after a hectic day. If you are a sommelier or a wine-consumer with some degree of wine expertise, chances are you will focus on deconstructing and analysing the wine on its aroma, appearance, acidity and so on. Doing this, is likely to undermine or numb your feelings and emotional experience towards the wine and its consumption. In contrast, if you are a lucky novice, you would simply savour the wine with spontaneity and experience more intense emotions and feelings from its consumption. One can visualise similar experiences in consumption domains of music, photography, movies and so on.

Does this imply that in case of such products and fields, expert-consumers are doomed to experience emotional numbness? The answer, thankfully, is in the negative.

So, does it mean that our sommelier too can enjoy a glass of wine, to experience wholesome positive feelings and emotions? The answer, thankfully, is in the affirmative.

The research mentioned above suggests that experts can escape the emotional numbness trap, when they need to, by leaning themselves away from a knowledge-driven analytical approach to assess their consumption experiences. Instead such expert-consumers can deliberately shift their focus towards the feelings and emotions emanating from their consumption experience.

So, whether you are a celebrity chef or a discerning food reviewer, the next time, you head out with your friends to enjoy a meal at a popular Dhaba, follow a simple trick. Make sure that the analytical expert within you is fast asleep, and allow your feelings and emotions be fully spiced up.

(This is an updated and revised version of an article first published on cnbctv18.com in April 2021)

6. It's okay to be selfie-centred

The lure of the self, myself, oneself is a potent one. There were times when most cultures looked down upon its members eulogising themselves for possessing great looks, intellect, wit, creativity, etc.

Today, each one of us has a self-love tool in our hands created by the Smart Ones who knew that humans love to love themselves. Therefore, 'Selfies' made possible by modern human being's greatest addiction, the mobile phone.

No longer does one need to hide one's love for thyself. Taking and sharing selfies is recognised as a right even by governments and public authorities the world over. It is not uncommon to find 'Selfie Spots' at tourist locations, much like we have designated spaces for nursing mothers.

Take the case of the designated 'Selfie Points' now created at every curated publicity event and at popular tourist venues. In New Delhi, when in late 2018 the local Government opened a newly made bridge over the river Yamuna, the 'Selfie Point' was part of the offering. In the initial days there was a mad rush as citizens exercised their right to take selfies at the iconic new structure, at times risking a possible accident such as falling off the bridge into the river.

Indeed, they have a right to show the world, that is, their Instagram pals and Facebook friends, most of whom they have never met — Hey, I made it. The 'I' being in bold letters.

While selfies have assumed widespread acceptability in the modern world, some critics and psychologists have raised warning signals against this mode of self-presentation.

(Photo: Unsplash/Priscilla Du Preez)

Few years ago, a hoax story in media reported about Selfitis, 'the obsessive-compulsive desire to take photos of one's self and post them on social media as a way to make up for the lack of self-esteem and to fill a gap in intimacy', as a mental disorder recognised by the American Psychiatric Association. Though the story was untrue, it did not stop academics from exploring and measuring the selfie phenomenon.

Psychologists argue that taking selfies is a self-oriented action, which allows users to establish their individuality and self-importance.

Selfie obsession has also been associated with narcissism. Do we really think of selfie-takers as selfish, self-loving shallow beings?

In an interesting research, users of selfie sticks were perceived by others as less socially attractive, moderately narcissistic and moderately inconsiderate. Although there is a strong argument that narcissism has a positive effect towards taking selfies, other researchers have found no relationship between selfie-taking and narcissism. Other reasons have also been attributed to the strong desire to take selfies such as to provide a greater appeal to others in their social media space, attention-seeking loneliness and being self-centred.

But selfie-taking and sharing behaviour may not always be a shallow way for teenagers, youth and celebrities to display narcissism and fashion, seek attention and practice self-promotion.

For many, selfies could be the means to fulfil their desires for equity, power and confidence, motivated by the strong desire to escape censorship, express true selves and to overcome illiteracy. For instance, research with urban slum-dwellers in Brazil revealed that selfie-taking and sharing was a means for the youngsters to escape their constrained life situations, and to communicate and truly express themselves.

Thus, socio-cultural context may profoundly influence an individual's motivations behind taking and sharing selfies. So, the next time you see an adolescent or a youngster taking a selfie in the middle of a crowded road with stray cows or in front of any grand structure, do not instinctively dismiss that person as a self-loving, self-obsessed millennial. That selfie may be that person's sought-after means to experience freedom and self-expression.

(This is an updated and revised version of an article first published in Economic Times, India in April 2019)

Brands

Randss

7. Brands' action plan in the times of COVID

As the world fought the COVID-19 epidemic with unprecedented lockdowns, they were also also important days for the brand managers to act, reflect and plan. Like everyone else, brands (brand managers) too found themselves stuck in the midst of a new paradigm. People were confined to their homes, markets and offices were closed, and consumption meant consuming the bare essentials.

Given such a scenario, how should have brands strategised? Should they have lied low, stopped advertising and saved the marketing rupees? Should they have prepared for the planned brand extension? With uncertainty being the new normal, no clear answers were available. Yet, nothing would have done a greater disservice to a brand and its stakeholders than for a brand to adopt a somewhat intuitive state of lethargy and inaction.

Tough times demand the best out of the great brands. And great brands have no option but to remain invested and seen to be invested in their stakeholders viz. customers, employees, suppliers and society. While, what brands do or can do depends on their type and business category, four action plans for brands are suggested for tough times such as those of the COVID pandemic:

empathise with authenticity, advertise the relevant, perform to serve and research to prepare.

Empathise With Authenticity

Tough times are occasions for great brands to display empathy towards their customers, suppliers, employees and society at large. This can take different forms — top managers cutting back on their remuneration to ensure that wages and jobs of employees are least impacted, making donations to funds (e.g., those meant to fight COVID-19), allowing buyers the needed time to pay their dues and so on. Important in all such actions is the element of authenticity. These actions should not be seen by others as an exercise in PR or brand building.

The fundamental rule is to do good to the world in a somewhat understated manner and with humility. When a brand shows a genuine concern for its stakeholders, the world will eventually notice and acknowledge. Such brands will be remembered for their goodness when it mattered the most — the best possible marker of a truly great brand.

Advertise The Relevant

During the pandemic, we observed a sharp decline in advertising on print media and TV. However, brands could have actually stepped in and supported the fight against COVID-19 through sensitive and relevant advertising. And some brands did so indeed. No doubt, this suited some brands (such as hygiene related brands, FMCG brands) more than others (say, a luxury car brand), but there is always some room for all types of brands to communicate the right messages.

Nike for instance, launched an advertisement with a tagline 'Play Inside, Play for the World'. Hygiene brands such as Dettol advertised to encourage cleanliness and health. And then there is an example of India's very own brand, Amul, which launched a series of interesting advertisements encouraging work-from-home and other required behaviours.

Surely, brand advertising need not succumb to the assault of tough times such as the pandemic. Certain brands, can and should continue with their usual advertising even in trying times, with due modifications to media spends and plans as may be warranted. And brands in a large variety of categories should consider relevant public service advertising which serves both the brands and their stakeholders.

Perform To Serve

For several brands, tough times present an occasion to show care and to make a difference through their performance. Take for instance, the crucial role played by online learning platforms around the world. With school and colleges shut, these e-learning providers had a business opportunity rooted in the possibility of service. It was a time when great brands in this domain emerged and stood out. Could they provide the right content? Could they enter into right tie-ups? Could they price their products keeping in mind the financial hardships? Could they provide a customer experience such that post-epidemic too the customers stayed with them?

Harvard Business Review made its coronavirus related content free, *Amar Chitra Katha* offered the digital version of its comics free and so on. Online businesses had a unique opportunity to serve people locked in their homes and highlight their sense of social responsibility. And indeed, they had an opportunity to convert millions into their long-term customers, and many were able to do the same.

Meanwhile, performance-based serving opportunities emerged for brands in a somewhat different way. When LVMH, the French luxury giant, manufactured sanitisers to meet the growing demand from health workers and people, it too performed to serve and added to its brand image.

Research To Prepare

Experts believe that COVID-19 threat is not yet over. Rising cases in China and elsewhere attest to the same. When we finally win over the virus and bring a full stop to the pandemic, the world we have is likely to be different from the one before. Consumers may think differently, spend differently and plan differently. Would they become more frugal? Would they cut down on luxury spending? Would they order more stuff online at their homes and offices and venture out less? Would big malls and supermarkets be less frequented? Would movie watchers, keep away from big-screen theatres in favour of home-watching on Netflix and Amazon Prime?

Consumer mindset, attitudes and behaviours are always evolving but events like the COVID-19 epidemic can change them significantly and for a foreseeable future. Brands need to be aware of customer attitudes, how they are thinking and how they may behave.

The evolving world will be very different and brands must invest now in marketing research to make better sense of the future realities than their competitors.

Brands must remember that the epidemic hit them and their competitors equally hard. So as they wish to recover, what will matter is the brand's speed and direction vis a vis its competitors.

A timely investment in marketing research can become a brand's competitive advantage. For instance, if research by an apparel brand suggests a strong increase in online purchasing, then the brand can invest in its online business capabilities viz. upgrade its software, re-train its off-line staff for greater online business, hire the required talent and so on.

If an automobile major expects trading down by customers from its higher-end to medium range models, it needs to plan its brand strategy accordingly. If movie-watching habits are set for a major change, then producers and distributors may need to work out imaginative solutions based in co-branding, collaborations and innovative partnerships.

Summing Up

It is true that the pandemic was unlike any other event we have witnessed in living memory. It brought economic activity and consumption to a sudden halt and the world economy is still in the recovery phase. In such times, it is the brands that take the right actions will emerge as winners in the post pandemic period.

These will be brands that have empathised with their stakeholders during the tough times, communicated with them on issues that mattered to them, performed in order to serve the customers and society when it was needed the most, and ones that will keep making an earnest effort to understand evolving customer attitudes, needs and realities.

(This is an updated and revised version of an article first published on cnbctv18.com in April 2020)

8. The coronavirus: will it fundamentally alter who we are and how we are?

Our world witnessed unprecedented times during the COVID-19 pandemic. While the worst seems to be over, the tell-tale signs of the virus are still witnessed in places around the world. A tiny virus, invisible to the naked eye, has impacted humanity in a manner unknown to generations. While disasters, wars and diseases are not new to us, COVID-19's spread and impact has been so wide that it has united countries and continents for a common cause like never before in our living memory.

The virus pitched its flag on a territory larger than that held by the mightiest kings in human history and its writ changed life everywhere from the crafted lanes of Paris to the enterprising streets of Mumbai. Millions of articles, papers, commentaries and WhatsApp messages informed and advised us on what COVID-19 meant, how to beat it and how to lead our lives in the midst of the pandemic. Nothing else mattered as the virus so very seamlessly and rapidly entered our minds and way of life.

Experts debated the virus's impact on economies and businesses and many presented a worrying scenario. Manufacturing was hit, trade and commerce came to a halt, daily-wage earners, professionals, taxi operators, hotels and tourism industry, small and big shop keepers, service providers and even beggars — all felt the squeeze unleashed by the spreading virus. The impact varied from country to country — some have been assaulted badly while others are mindful of what might still be in store. What worries is that the virus is still not out and efforts to defeat the virus carry on in research labs around the world.

There is little doubt that we humans shall eventually succeed and beat this virus. Already life as we knew in pre-COVID times has resumed in large parts of the world. Many see a silver lining and count on the virus to yield some worthy positive externalities: greater sensitivity towards mother nature, stronger bonds with our loved ones, sense of gratitude for what we have. Well-meaning Facebook posts by self-styled philosophers claim that the virus has tamed the wild human ego, made us aware of our mortality and it is exhorting the earth's most powerful species to slow down.

A Time For Reflection

The virus, it is argued will make us reflect upon some fundamental and universal truths; these are truths about our impermanence, our fragility and our oneness with nature and other beings. As compelling and intuitive as it may sound, will such a prognosis for the human race mellowing and slowing down materialise in reality? It is still too early to say, but if this happens, it would mean that, we the human beings will temper our needs and consumption, reassess our money-making urges and shun the environment-damaging materialism as a way of life. Instead, we will cherish and focus on what we already have — our families and relations, community and social bonds, nature's bounty and our beautiful planet. We can try to peep into the crystal ball based on the evidence we have on the platter.

Disasters and catastrophes that bring death and destruction make us aware of our impending mortality and reflect on our ways of being. If you have ever been to a crematorium following the death of your family member or a friend, you will probably recall how that experience revealed death to you as something imminent and real in a clear, stark manner. Perhaps, for some moments or more, it had made you realise how the quest for worldly success, material accumulation and wealth is eventually a meaningless one. Similar realisations also confront us when we experience more global and collective setbacks.

Take for instance, the 9/11 terror attacks that had stunned the world into disbelief. In particular, they shook millions of Americans who experienced existential threat and thoughts of death like never before. In the days that followed, attendance at Churches rose and people sought comfort in the safety of relationships and community. But did it slow down the American Dream premised in material success and the desire to have it all?

A month after the disaster, President George W. Bush while addressing the nation asked Americans to conduct business as usual and to go out shopping. And indeed they did. Consumption soared in the US in the following months with homes and cars being bought in record quantities and there was a rise in demand for appliances, electronics and so on.

Psychologists believe that the salience of their mortality and the existential anxiety it engenders motivates people to fill their life with meaning and derive self-esteem from their deep-rooted cultural beliefs about the nature of reality. And because materialistic consumption was a dominant cultural value for many Americans and a key ingredient of their worldview, they drew self-esteem and meaning in consumption which became a tool to mitigate their existential threats.

Spiritual Versus Material

Research by consumer psychologists have shown that thoughts of one's death and mortality results in positive attitude for luxury products and impulsive buying. Admittedly, most such findings emerge from studies in western countries and arguably the world of the orient is still a different one. We in India, for instance, claim to possess a spiritual focus so that our cultural values are not centred on consumerism and materialism.

Let us stay with India and the psychological impact of COVID-19 in an era of 24X7 coverage from across the world: has this virus made our mortality salient to us and spur us away from material goals towards more spiritual ones? Or, have we Indians indulged ourselves and shopped our way out of our anxieties?

Personally, even the grief, salience of my mortality and worldly detachment caused by loss of my dear relatives and friends, had at best, kept me away from the shopping malls for just a few days. It did not result in me buying any less than before though I simply don't remember if I bought any more. The data on revival of consumer spending in India post the worst phase of the pandemic suggests that there are more people like me out there than not. It seems that we humans are hard-wired to focus only on imminent threats, and thus it will be difficult for a death reminder or a grave threat gone-by alone to fundamentally change our way of life beyond a short time span.

In other words, we will most likely, remain as materialistic and as spiritual as we already are. Yes, there may be learnings that will make us wiser; in what ways, for how long and to what end, continues to be a matter of conjecture.

(This is an updated and revised version of an article first published on cnbctv18.com in March 2020)

9. Corona, kirana and the convergence model for Indian retail

The pandemic and several weeks of lockdown hit automobiles, construction, transport, tourism, trade and hospitality sectors extremely hard. It was no different for India's almost trillion-dollar retail sector, but segments of it remained active throughout the lockdown. While neighbourhood grocery or Kirana stores remained in business, the e-commerce companies were permitted to deliver essentials. In lockdown 3.O even the non-grocery standalone shops in residential areas were permitted to operate.

Most pundits acknowledge that amidst lockdowns the neighbourhood Kirana shops stood out for providing essentials to millions of citizens. With their last-mile reach, these stores were best placed to serve communities across cities, towns and villages. Much like sanitation workers, doctors, nurses, local bodies and police, the neighbourhood Kirana stores gained substantial citizens' respect.

Here was a non-glitzy grocery shop, a shopkeeper and his helper, opening their store daily to serve customers who, for a change, queued-up to shop. Customers, even those accustomed to spending their weekends shopping in mega malls or over their screens seemed satisfied, perhaps even happy with their neighbourhood Kirana store.

Overlooked were the small shops' hitherto ridiculed practices of selling goods at MRP, cash-only sales, pushing cheap candies in lieu of coins and offering limited choice. Millions of such stores belong to India's unorganised retail sector, which accounts for 80-85 percent of India's retail market share. They command over 90 percent of the food and grocery segment, which makes for 65-70 percent of India's total retail sales.

(Photo: Unsplash/Safal Karki)

Regardless of the above numbers, for much of the last decade, it is the fast-growing organised big retail and e-commerce which seized the attention of investors, analysts, policy-makers, middle class, business students and media. During the days of lockdown though, the mundane Kirana stores were noticed for their efficacy, value and access to communities and customers. In contrast, new-age shopping malls located at a distance from residential areas and designed to operate with large footfalls were not amenable to mandated restrictions and norms of social distancing.

These experiences make us ponder if a business model based on partnership with neighbourhood grocery stores could enable organised retailers (both big retail and e-sellers) to rapidly expand their customer base in India's food and grocery segment. Moreover, as this segment is somewhat inelastic to income variations and business cycles, increasing its contribution to overall sales can help organised retailers to hedge for demand volatility. As per a Boston Consulting Group report, the small stores across India shall remain relevant for a long time owing to what they offer: familiarity, proximity and the convenience of monthly credit.

The question remains: will India's retail sector witness collaborations between organised retailers and the neighbourhood stores? Let us consider the recent announcements of collaborations in India's retail sector. In 2020 Amazon tied-up with Future Group with an aim to boost Amazon's business in India's grocery segment and enable Future Retail's Big Bazaar stores to move rapidly on the 'offline to online' strategy. This tie-up that has ended up in arbitration, was not intended to include small Kirana stores as partners. Rather, it was an alliance between an e-commerce giant and a big offline retailer to take on other organised retailers as well as the neighbourhood Kirana stores. The same was true of Walmart's $16 billion acquisition of a majority stake in Flipkart in 2018.

In contrast, in 2020 Facebook invested $5.7 billion to acquire an almost 10 percent stake in Reliance's Jio Platforms, and this deal promised something different. The strategy suggested a possible partnership between big business (Jio Platforms, Reliance Retail-JioMart, Facebook) and millions of small Kirana shops across the country. The venture, it was said, would enable millions of WhatsApp users to order their groceries from neighbourhood stores via a WhatsApp message. Today, all major retail players, Amazon, Flipkart, Reliance Retail are competing to woo the Kirana shops to gain an upper hand in India's retail market. The model based on the convergence of big retail, small neighbourhood stores and e-commerce is making itself omnipresent.

Such convergence will be truly disruptive for India's retail sector and result in a win-win for four key stakeholders —

big retailers, e-sellers, small stores and the customers. It can enable wider use of technology and IT in managing the supply chain, working capital, inventory and customer needs. It can help create thousands of jobs in supply chain, technology and logistics while supporting millions employed by the Kirana stores. Such a convergence would discourage off-the-book business transactions and boost government tax collections. And finally, let us hope that such inclusive collaborations will help preserve the invaluable social capital accruing from relationships that emerge between a neighbourhood and its small stores, which in turn, are integral to a community's folklore, culture and history.

(This is an updated and revised version of an article first published on cnbctv18.com in May 2020)

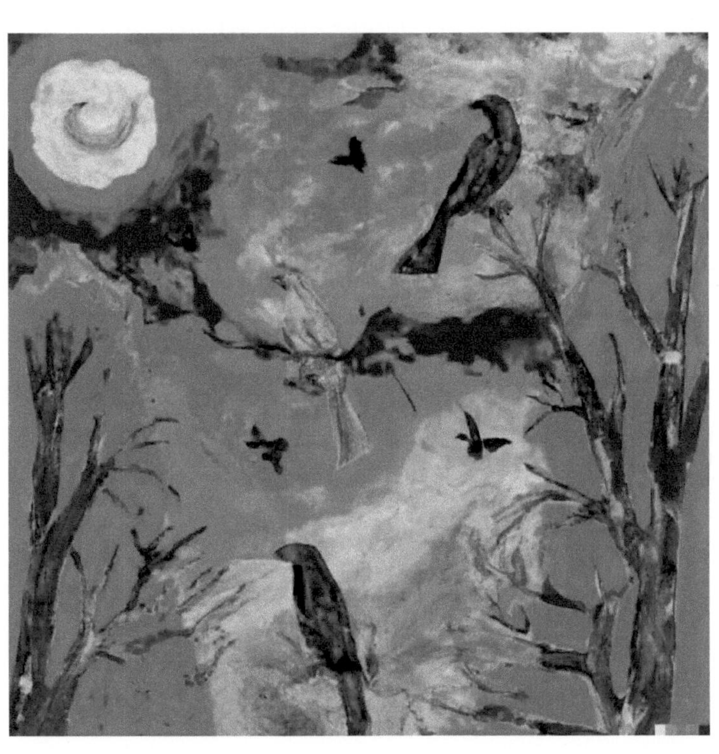

10. The pandemic's payoff: Seizing the green opportunity

In 2021, India's biggest company announced a Rs 75,000 crore (over $10 billion) investment in green energy over a three-year period.

Elsewhere, responding to a survey by *US Cotton Trust Protocol* and *Sourcing Journal*, over 40 percent of the participating global sustainability executives from the apparel industry revealed that the pandemic had positively influenced their future commitments to sustainability. Other studies reveal that the pandemic has fuelled demand for organic food in many markets. Governments, in several countries, have announced recovery plans with a strong focus on green projects in clean energy, public transportation and clean tech.

(Photo: Unsplash/Maxim Hopman)

'Going Green' is the common theme in these recent news and findings. Are we set on a path of greening our economies, businesses and consumption? The pandemic has certainly chiselled a sentiment for pro-environment disruptions. Two factors have helped.

First, the pandemic has enhanced our awareness about the magic of nature. During lockdowns, we noticed with awe, the clear blue skies, mountain ranges visible from long distances, flamingos flocking on a big city beach, wild animals reclaiming urban spaces and more. Return of nature, was a theme of conversations in homes, on news channels and social media.

Second, the pandemic motivated a shift towards a more collectivist worldview. 24x7 news and visuals of deaths heightened peoples' realisation about their own mortality and enhanced their anxieties. This, along with economic hardships, shortages and uncertainty made people seek refuge in relationships, in sharing and in helping and caring for others. Research too supports this change. In a big data study, published in *Human Behavior and Emerging Technologies* journal, psychologists Noah FG Evers, Patricia M Greenfield and Gabriel W Evers analysed content from google searches and social media posts on Twitter, internet forums and blogs in the USA. They noted a strong shift towards collectivist values in the USA after the pandemic was declared a national emergency in March 2020. Such a shift in values, they suggest, is consistent with predictions based on Patricia M Greenfield's *Theory of Social Change, Cultural Evolution, and Human Development.*

However, the shift towards collectivist values may not be limited to just one country or society. Think for yourself—did you experience an enhanced urge to help others? Did you feel more connected to your families, friends and neighbours? Importantly, the above value shift also has pro-environment implications. The collectivist rather than individualist values (and societies) are more consistent with pro-environment attitudes and behaviours.

These pandemic-induced factors seem to have enhanced the awareness and support for pro-environment institutional actions, consumer behaviour and way of life. A survey by Ipsos revealed that more than 70 percent respondents from across the world considered climate change over time as serious a crisis as COVID-19. The numbers for China (87 percent) and India (81 percent) were even higher. The majority of respondents favoured a green economic recovery. Another study by Kantar suggested an increase of over 20 percent (2020 vs. 2019) in the percentage of 'Eco Actives', a term it uses for consumers who are high on environmentally conscious consumption.

The pandemic did boost the pro-environment attitudes, backed and prodded by a collectivist worldview. This would suggest a rising demand—a big of part of it, still latent—for green products and services. It is a moment that must be seized by businesses to adopt the triple bottom line—people, planet, and profits—mandate.

Businesses need to make sustainable innovation a part of their very DNA. They must align their structure, processes, and outputs to minimise their carbon footprint; strive to become carbon neutral. It is an opportune time to adopt green technologies, alter supply chains, re-educate workforce and modify product life cycles. This should help create a strong portfolio of eco-friendly products and services to satisfy environmentally-conscious consumers.

For businesses' green shift to succeed, marketing managers role would be key. For in the final analysis corporates' green investments would be guided by the stability and size of the pro-environment market and consumer demand. Marketing can help solidify consumers' preference for green options despite the availability of competing cheaper, less green alternatives. Through well-designed marketing and communication, the environment-friendly brands, products and services can be firmly positioned as the 'best' options. Creative marketing and communication can help strengthen the narrative favouring eco-friendly consumption and nudge consumers towards greener choices. Marketing's touchstone would be whether green alternatives become consumers' first choice and way of life.

The pro-environment paradigm has been brought into a sharper focus by a deadly virus, presenting us with a great opportunity. But this opportunity may not last for long. For Greenfield's Theory also predicts that post-pandemic, when mortality (and its salience) is lowered and economic prosperity returns, societal values will shift back to what they were. While we hope for pro-green values and behaviours to persist, a safer bet lies in governments and corporates exploiting the present-day soft corner for the environment, to invest in a sustainable future. With the right efforts, green consumption may come into vogue. In contrast, greenwashing or pseudo environment-friendly actions by corporates could greatly harm the cause. The change must be real and sincere. It will not be easy, nor will the results be immediate. But the journey must begin and begin now.

(This is an updated and revised version of an article first published on cnbctv18.com in June 2021)

11. Message of Mission LiFE: for a pro-planet lifestyle, the buck stops with us

The stage for a grand push to Mission LiFE was set as India's Prime Minister Narendra Modi was joined by United Nations Secretary General Antonio Guterres at Gujarat's Kevadia for a mega event in October 2022. Considering that this was UNSG's first India visit during his second term, it testified the mission's global appeal.

Henceforth, Mission LiFE will be India's signature initiative at the UN and other international platforms for showcasing climate action and early achievement of the Sustainable Development Goals.

So what is Mission LiFE? It all began in 2021 at COP 26 in Glasgow when Prime Minister Modi invoked a concept called LiFE, or Lifestyle for Environment. By doing so, he gave expression to a reality that the world has overlooked at great peril. We cannot continue to live the way we have been living. The 'use and dispose' lifestyle has to give way to habits reflecting a mindful planet orientation.

Later, India's Cabinet approved the country's updated Nationally Determined Contribution (NDC) that was communicated to the UN Framework Convention on

Climate Change. The first of the eight points listed in the updated NDC emphasises the need "to put forward and further propagate a healthy and sustainable way of living based on traditions and values of conservation and moderation, including through a mass movement for 'LiFE' as a key to combating climate change". During India's presidency of G20, sustaining and promoting LiFE will be among key focus areas for deliberations.

How sustainable is Mission LiFE? It envisages adoption of a circular economy through people's participation. It also plans to nurture a global network of individuals, namely 'Pro-Planet People' or P3,

(Photo: Unsplash/Angelo Pantazis)

who will have a shared commitment to adopt and promote environment-friendly lifestyles.

Niti Aayog and Ministry of Environment, Forest and Climate Change, in partnership with other institutions made a Global Call seeking ideas - to drive climate friendly behaviours among individuals, households and communities; for innovative solutions to promote wider adoption of traditional, climate-friendly practices or create livelihood options for communities who may lose their jobs with a shift towards climate-friendly production; and for scalable best practices to bring about climate friendly behaviour change.

Public, academic and private institutions were asked to submit idea papers by the end of 2022. The 100 best ideas shall become part of a compendium to be released at the Global LiFE Conference and the best ideas shall be awarded at the COP 28 to held in the UAE.

Ideas indeed can change the world. However, there is always an implementation challenge to be dealt with. But in this case, failure is not an option and the luxury of procrastination is simply not available. Adopting to a new LiFE would entail massive disruption necessitating ceasing of old habits and adopting new ones. It would demand a fundamental change to the way we lead our everyday lives, every minute and second. And changing behaviours is challenging, and sustaining change even more so.

A successful shift to LiFE requires focusing on three elements – a stakeholder-based approach, adoption of 'planet orientation' as a talisman, and sustained citizens' buy-in. Adopting a pro-planet lifestyle is no longer the responsibility of the 'other'. The buck stops at each one of us, be it institutions, nations, societies or individuals; or be they governments, corporations, entrepreneurs, universities and schools or NGOs.

Dogged engagement has been the vital ingredient for the success of the International Solar Alliance championed by India. Likewise, consider the recent ban on single use plastic in India. A stakeholder approach involving collaboration among industry bodies, manufacturers, scientists, schools and educational institutions, civil society groups such as RWAs, media, and local bodies has a better chance for evolving and diffusing sustainable alternatives to such plastics, generating awareness and sustaining the motivation to adopt plastic-free lifestyles.

For each stakeholder, 'planet orientation' has to become a talisman to judge its thinking, ideas and actions. The DNA of all policies and programmes, decisions, practices, functions, institutional and individual behaviours must be impregnated with a 'planet first' approach. Sustainability and preservation of the environment can no longer be the sole responsibility of just one ministry in a government or a sustainability division in a business house. Governments and multilateral institutions have to ensure that regulations, laws and public infrastructure encourages and mandates pro-planet business practices and citizen behaviours.

The world of business needs a green shake up too. Business performance, accounting and audit practices, HR norms and employee appraisals, production and R&D, packaging, marketing and distribution and all other functions must be assessed on the touchstone of planet orientation.

In the final analysis, success of LiFE would lie in the popular adoption of green behaviours by people, resulting in a mass movement for a planet friendly lifestyle. This is easier said than done as changing entrenched habits require much self-control, effort, willpower and mindfulness. Moreover, there shall always be reasons to carry on as usual. That being so, individuals, societies and even nations have to be nudged to imbibe planet orientation as a cherished personal value. For Mission LiFE to succeed, humanity's buy-in is a must.

Making planet orientation as a top-of-the mind personal value can instantly drive seemingly small but hugely impactful behaviour changes. It would make us switch off the appliances when not in need, use less water while brushing our teeth, be mindful of plastic consumption, dispose of our e-waste responsibly, walk or cycle to our neighbourhood markets and carry our own jute bag for shopping.

(This is an updated and revised version of an article first published on indianexpress.com in October 2022)

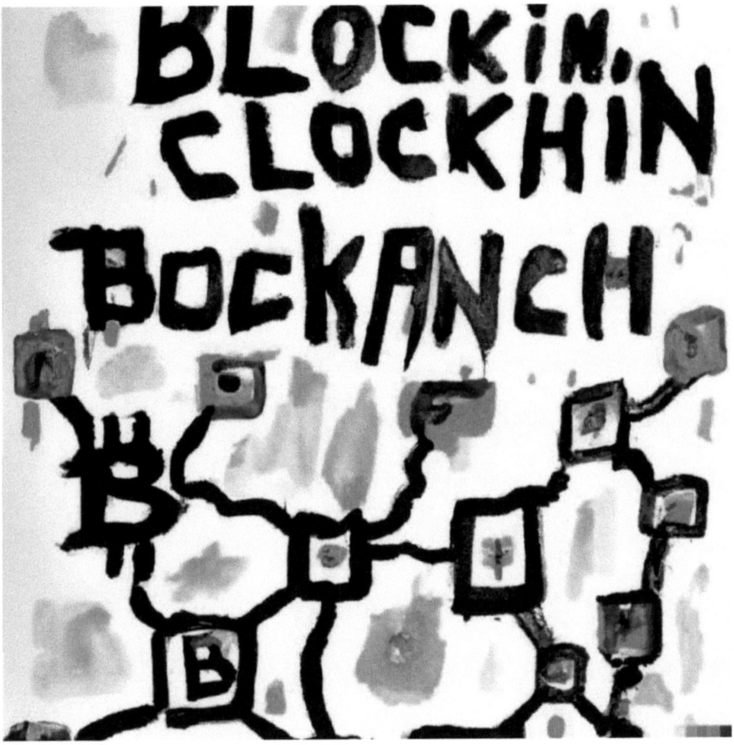

BLOCKIN.
CLOCKHIN
BOCKANCH

12. Exploring the blockchain's potential in education

Cryptocurrencies were in the news during much of 2022. But perhaps a bigger story lies in the blockchain technology that powers them. Globally, while the governments and banks grappled with the popularity of digital currencies, the potential of blockchain technology to transform other key sectors was seldom noted. One such sector this technology could truly revolutionise is education.

The pandemic affected educational institutions worldwide. While we hope that campuses would again buzz with the physical presence of students and teachers, the widespread use of digital technology in education is here to stay. Through blended learning and flipped classrooms, students are no longer limited by teaching resources and learning possibilities available within the institutions' physical boundaries. The new world is there for the taking – where knowledge from across the country and indeed the world can be availed.

With the National Education Policy 2020 (NEP-2020), India has set an ambitious agenda. The goal is to achieve 100 percent Gross Enrolment Ratio (GER) in school education by 2030 and double it in higher

education, to reach 50 percent by 2035. Our students, it is envisaged, will have increased flexibility and subject choices, with no rigid separations across disciplines. We need to invest in digital education and related technologies to achieve these ambitious targets, and to provide education that is holistic and multidisciplinary.

There are several aspects to making a robust Digital Education Ecosystem (DEE) - content development, teaching, evaluations, grading, attendance recording, achievements, certificates, degrees and diplomas. Stakeholders such as educational institutions, prospective employers, mentors and certification agencies can be integrated into a DEE. With greater digitisation, there is an inherent need for more secure and fool-proof systems that can track students' academic activities as well as provide the required information to all stakeholders. The blockchain can emerge as a viable solution to manage such an integrated DEE.

Blockchain derives its name from the digital databases or ledgers where information is stored as "blocks" that are coupled together forming "chains". An exact copy of the blockchain is available to each of the multiple computers or users who are joined together in a network and any new information added or altered via a new block is to be vetted and approved by over half the total users. With the advent of Internet of Things

(IoT), availability of cheap computing and internet services, blockchain technology can now facilitate innovations across a range of processes and applications requiring management, storage, retrieval and safety of vast and important information. These include management of information pertaining to financial transactions (as in case of cryptocurrencies), electoral voting, medical records, academic lessons, property ownership records and professional testimonials. A decentralized framework makes the system and the information stored therein fraud-proof, transparent and credible.

(Photo: Unsplash/Marvin Meyer)

Blockchain technology could provide an excellent framework to manage student records ranging from day-to-day information such as assignments, attendance and extracurricular activities, to information about degrees and colleges they have attended. It would be a secure system that ensures educational records remain immutable. These could be relied upon by prospective educational institutions and recruiters, who can be provided access to relevant records. Similarly, information about teachers can be safely stored and this would enable an educational institution to monitor faculty performance. The blockchain ledger would provide a time-stamped and tamper-proof record of faculty performance – attendance, student evaluations, number of students opting for their electives, research output and publications. These records could be linked to faculty appraisal systems, thereby ensuring greater accountability.

The NEP-2020 calls for introducing multidisciplinary education where students would be able to choose their own combination of major and minor subjects along with flexibility in course duration. Here too, blockchain can help implement such a multiple entry and exit structure. Further, students can be assured of the quality of teachers and educators. It could enable educators to display their certified Skill Badges, allowing students to opt for courses in an informed manner. Meanwhile, students too, especially those in higher education and research, can adopt Skill Badges to indicate their proficiencies. This would enable faculty to identify the right students for projects. A blockchain-based ecosystem could also be used to design a scholarship system incentivizing students to maintain consistency and achieve academic excellence.

The adoption of blockchain in education could help improve the efficiency of the education ecosystem and optimize the use of human and physical resources. While doing so, concerns such as data privacy, cost, scalability and integration with legacy systems will have to be addressed. Doing so is worth every penny as it would help usher in an educational system that is better equipped to handle higher enrolment while being secure, transparent, collaborative, creative and future ready.

(This is an updated and revised version of an article first published on indianexpress.com in December 2022. The co-author of the article is Dr Anirban Chakraborti is the Dean of School of Engineering and Technology, BML Munjal University).

Printed by Libri Plureos GmbH in Hamburg,
Germany